TEDDY
THE
TASTER

An I WONDER WHY Reader

HOLT, RINEHART AND WINSTON, INC.
New York   Toronto   London   Sydney

TEDDY THE TASTER

by Lawrence F. Lowery

Consultant, ABRAHAM S. FISCHLER
Illustrated by ED RENFRO

Copyright © 1969 by Holt, Rinehart and Winston, Inc.
All Rights Reserved
Printed in the United States of America
Library of Congress Catalog Card Number: 76-90448
SBN: 03-081189-9
90123   52   987654321

One rainy Saturday Teddy could not
think of anything to do. He started one
thing, then another. Nothing seemed
to interest him. So he wandered out to
the kitchen for a snack.

He had eaten the first half of his
mustard sandwich when his sister Jo
walked in.

"Can I have a bite?" she asked. So Teddy held out the sandwich to her. Jo bit off a piece. "Ugh!" she said. "That tastes terrible!"

"I think it tastes great," said Teddy defensively. "You don't know a good taste from a bad one."

Then both of them began to talk about foods that tasted good — or bad. They also began to taste various foods they found handy in the kitchen.

So it went. By the time Teddy's friend Marvin came over later in the afternoon, the talking and tasting had turned into a game.

Jo and Teddy had made up rules and had kept score. They told Marvin all about the game. Then the three of them played it.

Jo tied a cloth over Teddy's eyes. He could not see anything.

"Open your mouth," she directed. She put a piece of chocolate cookie on Teddy's tongue. "What is it?" she asked.

Teddy let the cookie rest on his tongue for a minute. Then he ate it. "Well,..." he thought out loud, "it's sort of sweet. It's something I like." He paused. He had only three guesses and he did not want to waste them.

On the second try he guessed, "Chocolate cookie."

"Right," Jo said and put five points next to Teddy's name on the score sheet.

Then Marvin's eyes were blindfolded
and he had a turn. He used up all his
guesses before he found out he was
tasting a carrot.

Jo did better. She guessed grape jelly
on the first try and won ten points.

The children played the tasting game for about an hour. During that time Marvin had not been able to guess any food correctly. Jo thought she and Teddy did better because they had had more practice. "No," said Marvin. "That's not it."

"I've been thinking," he went on, "that it is probably because of my cold. I've had a cold all week. I haven't been able to smell anything. And nothing tastes right to me.

"I usually can tell potato from apple," he finished. Marvin had guessed potato when Jo put a piece of apple on his tongue.

"Let's do something else," Teddy suggested. So they did.

Several days later Teddy was back in the kitchen. He was tasting food again. He tasted a slice of lemon. Then, holding his nose and keeping his eyes shut, he tasted the lemon again. He did not ask himself, "What is this?" or "Do I like this?" Instead he thought "What is this taste?" He pretended he had to tell someone what a lemon tasted like. "It tastes sour," he concluded.

Tasting food got to be a favorite game of Teddy's. It was something, too, he could play at mealtime. After a few weeks his father called him "Teddy the Taster." The rest of the family used that nickname whenever they thought of it. Teddy, as a matter of fact, rather liked it.

Teddy got to know the taste of many foods.
Salty pretzels,
sour pickles,
sweet candy, and
bitter almonds
were just some of Teddy's favorites.

Teddy liked a food if it had any of these tastes—salty, sour, sweet, or bitter.

Take the salty taste, for instance.
It was because of the salt that Teddy
liked roasted peanuts and pretzels. He
could eat salty crackers by the box, or
a whole bag of salty potato chips down
to the very last one. The salt he
sprinkled over the butter on hot, fresh
corn-on-the-cob he thought was great.

Sour foods made Teddy's mouth
water. They made his lips shut tight.
Sometimes they gave him a funny
feeling behind his ears. He liked this
sour taste.

Teddy liked sour apples, lemons, and
pickles and sour lemon candies. Teddy
could eat sour foods day or night.

Bitter foods have a dry and
unpleasant taste. At least that's
what some people thought. Not Teddy.
He liked that taste, but not in large
amounts. So Teddy ate only small
pieces of bitter baking chocolate. It
was the only time he was satisfied with
a small serving.

Best of all Teddy liked the taste of
sweet foods. He just loved
candy
cookies
iced cupcakes
and the sugar coated doughnuts that
his mother baked.
　Whenever sweet foods were around,
so was Teddy the Taster.

Now Teddy is becoming an expert on tastes. He is not trying to find out if this tastes good or if that tastes better. Every food tastes good to him.

Teddy asks, instead, "Does this taste sour? Or is it sweet? Maybe it's bitter? I know it's not salty."

Many times he decides whatever he is testing, or tasting, is a combination of tastes. This morning he tested a grilled cheese sandwich.

Now Teddy is testing a double chocolate ice cream cone. What will he decide? Maybe he will decide to have a second test.